2/91

Date Due

SEP 2 9 2012		
SEP 2 5 2013		

Do You Know?

THE

STORY OF FLIGHT

By
Jim Robins

Warwick Press
New York/London/Toronto/Sydney
1986

Contents

The story of flight begins in the days of myth and legend, when only a few gods and super-heroes were thought to be able to fly. For ordinary humans, flight was a baffling mystery. On land, they could walk and run with the animals; in the sea they could float and swim with the fishes. In the meantime the birds soared overhead with seemingly effortless ease, while all people could do was stand back enviously and wonder.

It was not until the last century that the mystery of flight was solved. The secret did not lie in magic, or in god-given powers — but in science and the properties of air. This book shows how the trials and triumphs of the early airmen led to the high-speed air travel we take for granted today.

ISBN 0-531-19022-6

Library of Congress Catalog Card No. 86-50786

Published in 1986 by Warwick Press 387 Park Avenue South, New York, New York 10016.
First Published in 1986 by Grisewood and Dempsey Ltd., London
Copyright © by Grisewood and Dempsey Ltd., 1986
Printed in Spain.

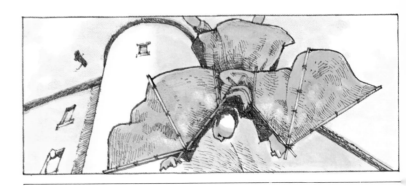

① Birdmen And Balloonists

The most famous of all the "birdmen" were Daedalus and his son Icarus. Greek legend tells of their daring escape flight from Crete, using feathers stuck to their arms with wax. They flapped bravely through the air, but their flight ended in tragedy when Icarus soared too near the sun. As his wax wings melted, he plunged to his death in the seas below.

The sad fate of Icarus did not put the birdmen off. For hundreds of years, people clung to the belief that they could fly by simply flapping their arms. Their home-made wings of wood and fabric usually took them in one direction only — straight downward.

These struggles provided some entertainment for a cruel and jeering public, but did little to help the scientific understanding of flight. The careful studies of Leonardo da Vinci came closer to solving the problem. But as it turned out the first real flight was not to come about from copying the birds at all.

In 1709, at the Portuguese court, Laurenço de Gusmao trapped hot air in a model balloon and made it rise up in the surrounding colder air. The court was impressed, until the model lost control and damaged a pair of royal curtains.

In 1782 in France, Joseph and Etienne Mongolfier noticed that burning pieces of paper rose upward in a fire. Not realizing that hot air is lighter than cold, they put this down to a mysterious gas in the smoke. They went on to launch the first large hot-air balloon, piloted by an alarmed sheep, duck, and cockerel.

The Mongolfiers built a magnificent new balloon for the first manned flight in history. Throughout the journey the fire under the balloon needed constant stoking by one of the two passengers. A safer means of flight came with the invention of the hydrogen balloon, which lifts because hydrogen is lighter than air.

② Learning To Fly

Birds fly because wind passes over their curved wings, providing the *lift* that raises them off the ground. To move forward, the sculling action of their wings provides the force known as *thrust*.

By 1700, it had been realized that people were too heavy, and their muscles too weak, to fly like the birds. If people were to move through the air, the problems of lift and thrust had to be tackled separately. The first person to understand this was an Englishman named Sir George Cayley, who discovered in 1804 that the surface of a kite gave lift. He built a small glider by fitting a kite to the end of a long stick, adding a moveable tail for steering. It was a success, and Cayley went on to build full-sized gliders.

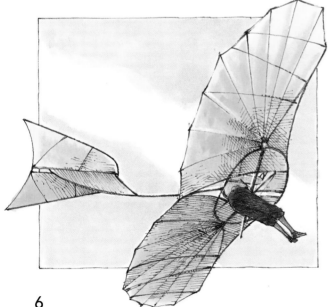

Cayley realized that a source of power was now needed to give thrust to his gliders. But at this time, no one had built an engine that was light enough or small enough. However, his inventions helped many other airmen to take to the skies. One of the most famous was a German mechanic called Otto Lilienthal, who made hundreds of glider flights using both *monoplanes* (using one set of wings like the one here) and *biplanes* (with two sets of wings). Swinging beneath his strange-looking machines, he learned a great deal about balance and steering.

6

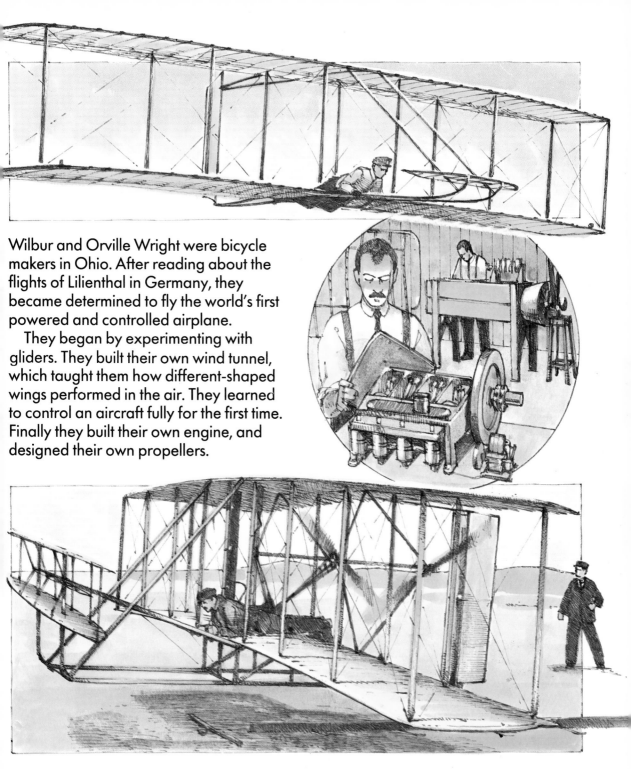

Wilbur and Orville Wright were bicycle makers in Ohio. After reading about the flights of Lilienthal in Germany, they became determined to fly the world's first powered and controlled airplane.

They began by experimenting with gliders. They built their own wind tunnel, which taught them how different-shaped wings performed in the air. They learned to control an aircraft fully for the first time. Finally they built their own engine, and designed their own propellers.

After four years of careful planning, and hundreds of glider flights, the Wrights were ready to test their first powered airplane. On December 14, 1903 *Flyer* took off into the air — and stalled.

Three days later they tried again. With Orville lying on the wings to control its tips, *Flyer* rose into the air for a bumpy flight lasting a whole 12 seconds. The age of powered flight had at last begun.

3 Convincing The World

D'AVIATION
REIMS ~ 1909 ~

To begin with, Europe was slow to follow the Wrights' example. Many people still refused to believe that powered flight was possible.

In 1909 a French pilot named Louis Blériot hit the headlines by making the first flight across the Channel. His success and others like it helped to wake up public interest, and later that year thousands of people flocked to the world's first great air show at Reims in France.

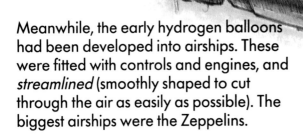

Meanwhile, the early hydrogen balloons had been developed into airships. These were fitted with controls and engines, and *streamlined* (smoothly shaped to cut through the air as easily as possible). The biggest airships were the Zeppelins.

When World War I broke out in August 1914, few people thought that aircraft could be much help in battle. But as planes could cross enemy lines with ease they soon became valuable for spying. Pilots took photographs of troop movements, occasionally dropping a few hand-held bombs before flying away. Soon they began to take potshots at other pilots with pistols and rifles. It wasn't long before the sky had also become a battlefield.

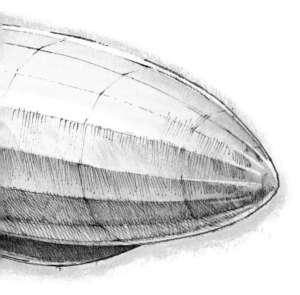

Within a year of the war aircraft were being fitted with machine guns. Fighter pilots fought alone or in formations. In battles called "dogfights," planes whirled and looped in order to fire a round of bullets at each other at close range. Few pilots had parachutes, and the death rate was high. Those who did survive became national heroes, or "aces." Most pilots flew biplanes, which could turn easily in the air and were stronger and easier to build than monoplanes. By the end of the war both types had more powerful engines and could carry more guns.

For the first time in any war ordinary citizens came under attack from the air. One of the most feared sights of the war was the appearance of the German Zeppelins, which could fly halfway across Europe to bomb undefended towns.

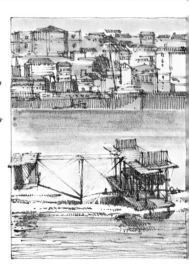

After the war pilots flew to every corner of the world. On May 16, 1919 three U.S. Navy flying boats left Newfoundland in an attempt to cross the Atlantic by air.

The 'boats had planned to break their journey at Horta in the Azores — about 1,200 miles away. Only two made it. The third crashed, and its crew had to be rescued.

Another of the 'boats limped into the harbor at Horta, but was unable to go any farther. The last of the three flew on alone, arriving at Lisbon in Portugal on May 27.

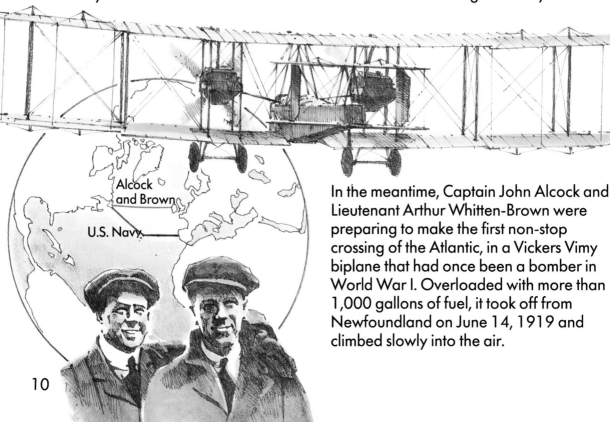

Alcock and Brown

U.S. Navy

In the meantime, Captain John Alcock and Lieutenant Arthur Whitten-Brown were preparing to make the first non-stop crossing of the Atlantic, in a Vickers Vimy biplane that had once been a bomber in World War I. Overloaded with more than 1,000 gallons of fuel, it took off from Newfoundland on June 14, 1919 and climbed slowly into the air.

For much of the journey, Alcock and Brown were lashed by sleet and snow in their open cockpit. Freezing fog made it almost impossible for them to see where they were going, while a broken radio cut them off from the ground. More than once, Brown was forced to climb onto the wing to hack ice away from the engines. Another time, Alcock found that the plane was flying upside down in thick cloud only 100 feet above the sea!

As they sighted the Irish coast and prepared to land, what had first seemed to be a smooth field turned out to be a bog. A safe but bumpy touchdown ended their historic 16-hour flight.

5 The Pathfinders

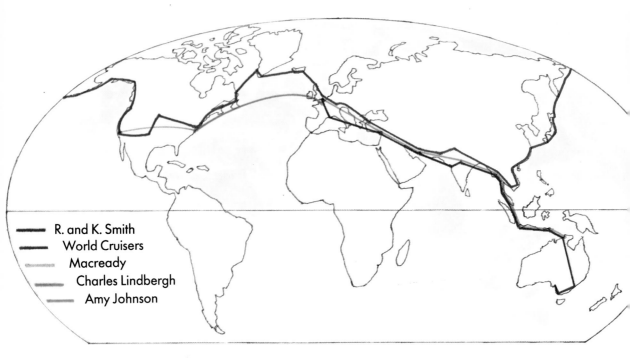

- —— R. and K. Smith
- —— World Cruisers
- — — Macready
- —▪▪▪— Charles Lindbergh
- —— Amy Johnson

At the start of the 1920s most people still thought of flying as a dangerous adventure. The great pioneer pilots helped to convince the public that airplanes were safe. Wherever they flew, passenger planes soon followed. And lessons learned on these test flights led to many improvements in aircraft design.

Ross and Keith Smith blazed the trail between England and Australia in 1919. Their Vickers Vimy battled through terrible weather conditions, and had to put up with many rough and ready airfields along the way. They reached Darwin after 28 days, winning $15,000 in prize money.

The first non-stop flight across North America was made in 1923, in a Fokker monoplane belonging to the U.S. Army Service. Lieutenants John Macready and Oakley Kelly flew between New York and San Diego in a journey that was to last 26 hours and 50 minutes.

In April 1924 four Douglas World Cruisers belonging to the U.S. Army Air Force set off on the first round-the-world flight. In a journey that took nearly 6 months, they stopped at the world's capital cities as well as many more exotic places. Today the journey can be done in 48 hours.

In 1927 an ex-stuntman and mail pilot called Charles Lindbergh made the first solo flight across the Atlantic. Seated behind huge fuel tanks, Lindbergh had trouble seeing out of his monoplane. His main problem was staying awake, but after 33½ hours he landed safely at Paris to a hero's welcome.

Amy Johnson became the first woman to fly solo from Britain to Australia in 1930. During an action-packed journey her tiny de Havilland Moth biplane survived a sandstorm in Turkey, a broken wing in Pakistan, and fierce Monsoon winds over Malaysia. She touched down at Darwin on May 24 after 20 days of flying.

6 Planes For Passengers

Where the pioneers had flown, passenger planes soon followed. The first of these were converted bombers. Passengers were fitted out with leather coats and goggles, and packed into the cockpit or uncomfortable cabins. Wherever they sat it was a cold and noisy flight.

Standards improved quickly. Airliners were specially built with comfortable cabins, and some began to serve refreshments during the journey. The noise level was kept down by building the engines onto the wings, away from the plane's main body or *fuselage* where the passengers sat.

One of the greatest airliners was the HP-42 series run by Imperial Airways. These were famous for their safety and reliability, and set new standards of airliner luxury in the 1930s.

The 1930s were the golden age of the flying boats. The boat-shaped hulls of these graceful planes allowed them to take off or land on stretches of water. At this time airports were few and far between, and land planes were often forced to stop at remote and hostile spots. Flying boats, on the other hand, could use the sea as a runway and make use of harbors all around the world. For many passengers they combined the thrill of air travel with the elegance of an ocean cruise. And as well as carrying 24 passengers, the 'boats took mail to all corners of the world.

Meanwhile, the giant Zeppelin airships continued to offer their passengers a first-class long-distance service. Then, in 1937 the huge *Hindenberg* was destroyed in a horrific explosion, killing 35 people. The public lost confidence in the airship, and services died out.

⑦ Progress In Peacetime

The 1930s were a time of great progress in aircraft design. One important change was the rise of the monoplane. This was greatly influenced by the aircraft that won the Schneider Trophy for seaplanes in 1931.

The beautiful streamlined Supermarine S6B monoplane set a new speed record of 400 miles an hour. The engine and general design of the Supermarine S6B later led to the Spitfire fighters of World War II.

While Britain was producing sleek racers like the Supermarine S6B, American designers were working on planes of a very different kind. For the National Air Races that took place every year, they built a series of monoplanes that were designed especially for speed and power over a very short distance. These barrel-shaped aircraft were highly dangerous machines, and many pilots lost their lives. However, many valuable lessons were learned about streamlining and power through racing competitions of this kind.

Designers packed the largest possible engines into the smallest possible air frames. The result was stubby-looking planes like the Gee Bees, which dominated the races in the early 1930s.

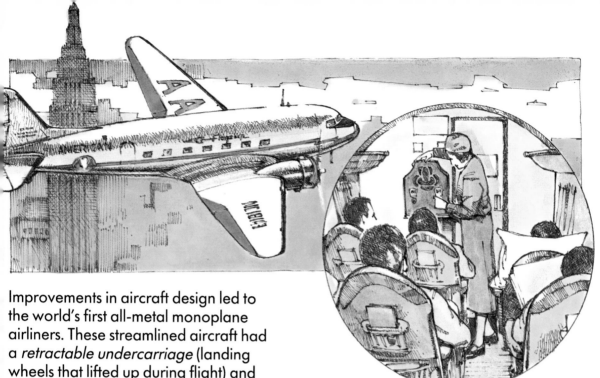

Improvements in aircraft design led to the world's first all-metal monoplane airliners. These streamlined aircraft had a *retractable undercarriage* (landing wheels that lifted up during flight) and an *automatic pilot* (a mechanical device that took over much of the pilot's work when the plane was in the air).

The most remarkable of the new airliners was the Douglas DC-3. More than 10,000 have been built since the 1930s, and many are still used today.

The DC-3 was built with a wider fuselage than previous models, allowing 20 passengers to travel in comfort. Some had sleeping berths for night travel, while soundproofing made in-flight entertainment possible for the first time.

Flying was still a rough and bumpy means of travel. To fly high enough to avoid the bad weather, aircraft had to be able to withstand the low air pressure that lay above the clouds.

In 1940 the Boeing Stratoliner opened a *pressurized* airliner service. By keeping the air pressure inside the aircraft constant, it was able to fly at a greater height or *altitude.*

⑧ Battle For The Skies

When war broke out again in 1939, there was no longer any doubt about the importance of warplanes. Alarmed by the size of the German Air Force in 1935, many other countries had been building up their air power. The British public knew what to expect when the air raid sirens droned overhead. As well as terrifying memories of the Zeppelins, the recent bomber raids made by Germany over Spain in the Spanish Civil War were fresh in people's minds.

In July 1940 the first battle ever to be fought entirely by airplane began. In an attempt to weaken Britain in preparation for an invasion, Germany sent squadrons of bombers to attack the southeast of England. Their planes were met by the two deadliest weapons of the Royal Air Force — the Hurricane and the Spitfire. Although they had 3,500 aircraft compared to the R.A.F.'s 704 fighters, the "Battle of Britain" ended in defeat for the German Air Force in September.

Fortunately for Britain, chains of *radar* stations had been set up along the east coast just before the Battle of Britain broke out. By beaming radio signals into the air, it was now possible to detect planes that were still a long way out of sight.

R.A.F. planes began to carry their own radar that produced an electronic map of the ground below and made night fighting much easier.

While the British specialized in night raids over German towns and cities during the war, the United States specialized in daylight raids against individual buildings. Special U.S. long-range fighters such as the P-51 Mustang were used to escort bombers sent on daylight raids over Germany.

The war in the Pacific carried on even after peace had been reached in Europe. In 1945 the B-29 Superfortress of the U.S. Air Force ended a series of raids on Japan by dropping atomic bombs on the cities of Hiroshima and Nagasaki. Thousands of people were killed, Japan surrendered, and a new age of nuclear menace began.

19

9 Jets And Rockets

Jet and rocket engines were developed during World War II. These burn fuel with oxygen to produce hot gases. The gases are then forced back out of the engine in order to drive the aircraft forward. The main difference between jets and rockets is that jets suck in air from outside the aircraft, while rockets carry their own oxygen supply. Some jets now use large *turbofan* engines to draw in extra air.

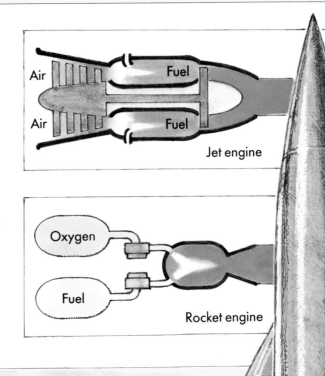

Air
Air
Fuel
Fuel

Jet engine

Oxygen
Fuel

Rocket engine

Heinkel 178

V-2

Jet engines were developed over a period of several years in both Britain and Germany. The first to fly was the German Heinkel 178, in August 1939. Later developments led to the world's first successful jet fighter, the Messerschmitt-262, and the jet bomber Arado-234. Both planes served during World War II.

A liquid-fuel rocket was used for the first long-range flying bomb, the V-2. Carrying explosives in its nose, the rocket flew high into the air before falling on targets hundreds of miles away.

Messerschmitt-163 Komet

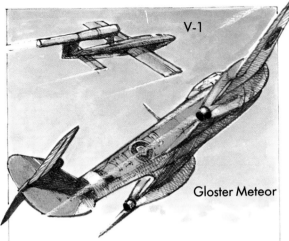

V-1

Gloster Meteor

The Messerschmitt-163 Komet was a German rocket-powered fighter plane, built to attack Allied bombers over Germany. It could fly at more than 490 miles an hour, but only carried enough fuel for a few minutes' flight.

The only British jet aircraft to see service in World War II was the Gloster Meteor twin-engined warplane. Here it is seen attacking a V-1 flying bomb which itself was powered by an early type of jet engine.

After the war, jets quickly replaced the slower propeller-driven combat aircraft. As speeds increased, the shape of the airplane changed to meet the demands of the powerful engines.

Although jet aircraft had appeared in World War II, they had never fought each other in the air. It was not until the Korean War of 1950–1953 that the first jet "dogfight" took place, when the Soviet MiG 15 fought the U.S. F-86 Sabre.

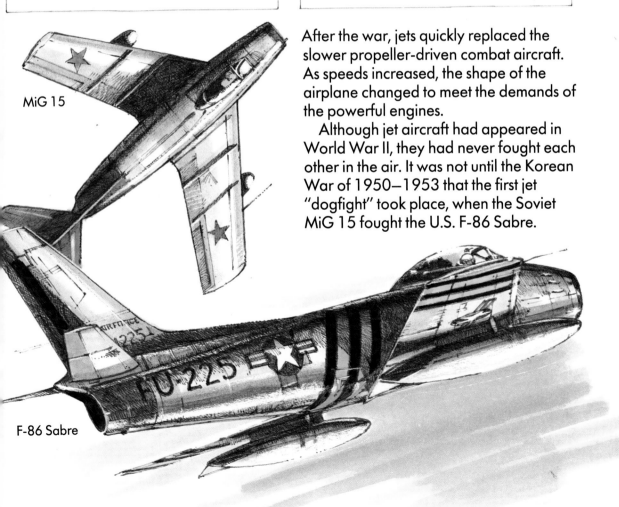

MiG 15

F-86 Sabre

⑩ Breaking Barriers

Jets were getting faster and faster — but there was still one major obstacle to be overcome.

Sound travels at around 730 miles an hour. For years, many scientists believed that no aircraft would be able to fly faster than this. They claimed that the plane would hit its own shock waves and be smashed to bits.

Among those who thought differently was a 24-year old U.S. Air Force pilot called Chuck Yeager. In 1947 he volunteered to fly a top-secret experimental rocket plane called the Bell X-1.

The tiny orange plane was carried beneath a Superfortress bomber. When it had reached an altitude of 3.7 miles, the rocket plane was launched and Yeager fired his liquid oxygen engines. The plane soared higher and higher as it approached the speed of sound. At 8 miles there was a slight bump. The "barrier" had finally been broken.

There was no hero's reception for Captain Yeager. His success was not made public until January 1948.

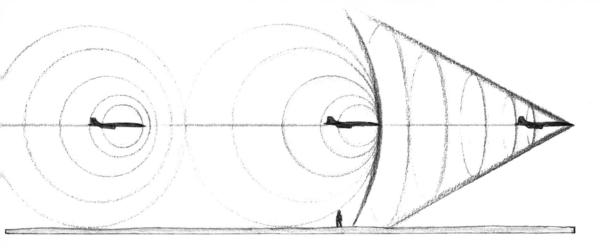

The round lines in the picture show the air disturbance caused by a plane. These are known as pressure waves. The waves travel at exactly the speed of sound (Mach 1).

As the plane reaches Mach 1, it catches up with the waves. The air ripples which had previously spread out ahead of it are pushed into a shock wave — the "sound barrier."

When the plane passes Mach 1, it pushes the tip of the wave into a cone shape. This increases the air pressure, which can be heard as a boom on the ground.

In the United States the search for supersonic power went even further with the X-15 rocket-powered plane. During a research program lasting between 1959 and 1967, the speed limit was pushed up to 4,534 miles an hour, or Mach 6.27—the fastest machine people have ever traveled in, apart from a spacecraft.

When the Soviet Tu-144 and the Anglo-French Concorde entered service in the mid-1970s, supersonic air travel became available to ordinary passengers. Today only Concorde is still in service. Its slim, dart-like shape is designed for high speeds, as straight wings would set up too much resistance to the air.

⑪ Jet Journey: 1

A modern international airport is as complicated and busy as a city. Every year millions of people pass through its doors while hundreds of thousands of planes take off and land.

As the passengers are checking in, their plane is serviced, cleaned, and refueled, while the crew discuss the route and weather conditions with the ground staff. Once they have boarded their plane, the crew wait for the go-ahead from Ground Control and Air Traffic Control. When the flight is cleared, the giant plane pulls away from the terminal and *taxies* to the end of the runway. After a final check with Ground Control, the captain turns onto the runway and opens the throttles. At breakneck speed, the aircraft roars along the runway toward takeoff.

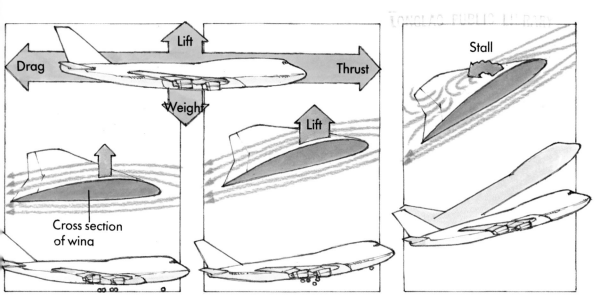

The secret of flight lies in the wing shape. As the plane speeds along, air flows more quickly over the curved top, causing a drop in air pressure which pulls the wings upward.

With engines at full power, the pilot lifts the plane's nose. As the angle to the flow of air increases, so does lift. This is more powerful than the plane's weight, so it takes to the air.

Climbing steeply, speed increases as the thrust of the engines overcomes *drag* (air resistance). But if the climb is too steep and too slow, lift is lost and the aircraft stalls.

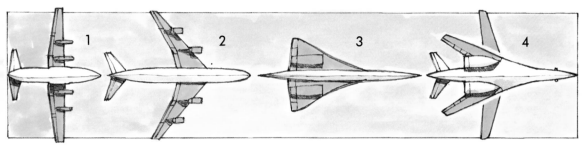

Straight wings (1) give good lift at low speeds, but cause a lot of drag at high speeds. *Swept wings* (2) cut down drag when the plane is flying fast, but need to be fitted with flaps and slats to improve lift at low speeds. The slender *delta wings* of Concorde (3) are ideal in supersonic flight, but make landing speeds very high. Ideally, wings would be able to change their shape during flight to meet different demands. Some modern combat aircraft now use this *swing-wing* device (4).

25

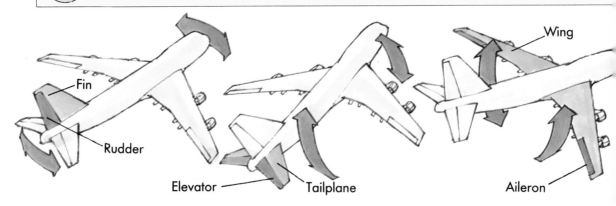

The tail's fin stops the aircraft from *yawing* from side to side. A rudder is hinged to the fin, which allows the pilot to control the plane's movement from side to side.

The tailplane stops the aircraft from *pitching* up and down. If the hinged elevators on the tailplane are up, the nose will rise, while putting them down causes it to dive.

The wings are angled upward at what is called the *dihedral angle*, to prevent the aircraft from *rolling*. Ailerons, hinged flaps in the wings, move up and down to control this.

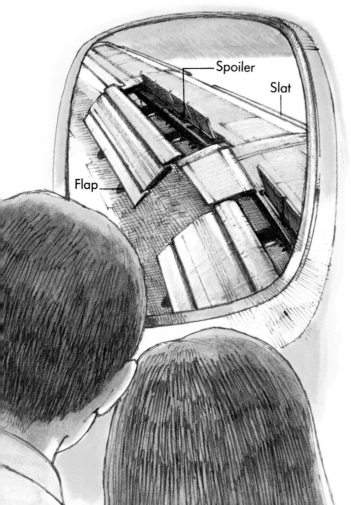

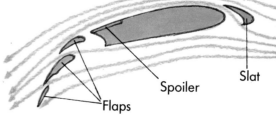

When the airliner takes off or lands, the shape of the wings changes dramatically. At the rear of the wing, called the *trailing edge*, are flaps which move backward and downward. At the front of the wing, or *leading edge*, are slats which move forward. These have the effect of making the wing broader and more curved, or *cambered*. The flow of air now has farther to travel over the wing, and so more lift is created. This allows the aircraft to take off sooner, or to land more slowly. When spoilers on top of the wings are raised, lift falls and the plane descends.

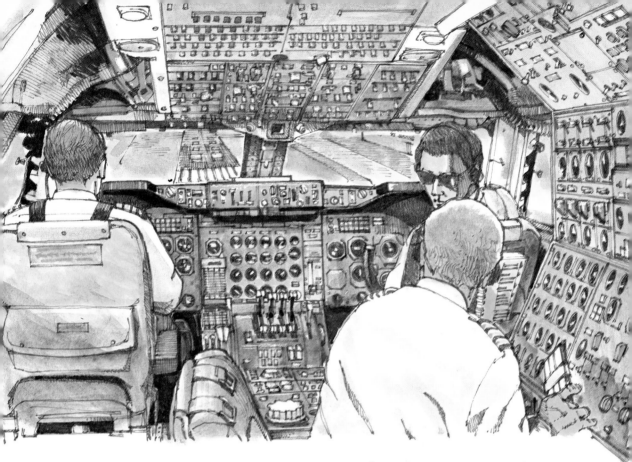

On the flight deck, the crew prepares to land. The Captain sits in the left-hand seat, the co-pilot on the right. In front of each are identical control wheels, rudder pedals, and flight instruments. Behind them is the flight engineer, who keeps a close check on all of the plane's systems.

After landing, the jet taxies up to its destination terminal. Long landing jetties reach out from the airport building to the aircraft's exit doors, to take the passengers to their checkpoints. Trucks of all sizes surround the plane, as preparations for the return journey begin.

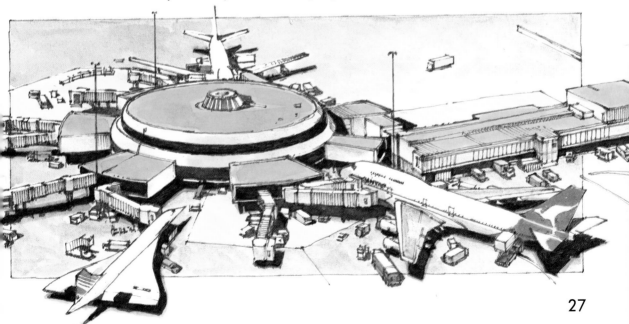

27

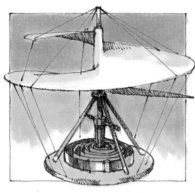

The first serious design for the helicopter was made by Leonardo da Vinci in the 1500s. Leonardo's design used a spiral wing, by which the machine screwed itself up into the air.

The *autogyro* was first built by Juan de la Cierva, in the 1920s and '30s. It had a normal engine and propeller for forward flight, but used a spinning wing, or *rotor,* to provide lift for short takeoffs.

The autogyro could not hover, nor could it take off straight up into the air, but it did lead directly to the first truly practical helicopter, designed by Igor Sikorsky between 1939 and 1942.

A helicopter can take off and land *vertically* (straight up or down) and can hover in mid air. Its rotor is driven directly by the engine, and not only lifts the machine but can be tilted to provide thrust forward, backward, and sideways. On single-rotor helicopters, a small side-mounted tail rotor stops the fuselage from spinning in the opposite direction to the main rotor.

Ordinary aircraft need long runways in order to build up enough speed to become airborne, or to land safely. Where there is no room for an airport in overcrowded cities, or where a military runway would be open to enemy attack, there is a need for an aircraft that can take off and land vertically.

3

2

1

The Harrier jump-jet can take off and land straight from woodland clearings or from the deck of a warship — yet it can also fly at nearly supersonic speeds.

The secret lies in its engine. Hot gases from the engine are forced through two nozzles on each side of the aircraft. When the nozzles are pointed downward (1), the Harrier is pushed upward into the air. The nozzles are then swung partly backward (2), pushing the aircraft forward until the wings can provide lift in the normal way. With the nozzles fully backward all the engine's thrust is used to move the plane forward. At the moment this type of aircraft is used only for military purposes. Another promising new development is the "tilt-wing" airplane, in which the whole wing, with its engines, tilts from the upright position at takeoff to a horizontal position for forward flight.

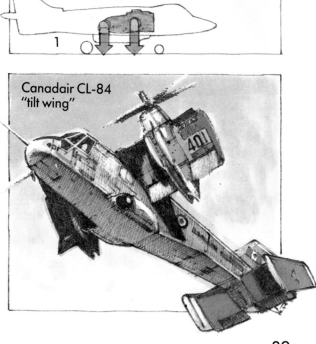

Canadair CL-84 "tilt wing"

⑭ New Frontiers

The hinged nose of the Lockheed C-5 Galaxy gapes open to allow 132 tons of cargo into its huge hold. Spanning about 220 feet, the Galaxy is one of the largest planes flying today. It is used for long-range transport by the U.S. Air Force.

The sinister-looking Blackbird is a spy plane for the U.S. Air Force. Flying at high altitudes at three times the speed of sound, its cameras can still focus on objects the size of a golf ball. Computers help the pilot to make split-second decisions in flight.

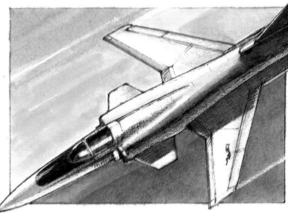

Some airmen have gone back to the idea of man-powered flight. In 1979 a lightweight plastic plane was pedaled across the English Channel by a young American called Bryan Allen. His journey took 2 hours and 20 minutes.

The most common design for supersonic aircraft is a slim, swept-back shape. However, recent test flights with the X-29 point the way toward swept-forward wings. These make it easier for the plane to twist and turn at high speeds.

Space travel is a very expensive business. Until the shuttle went into service in the 1980s, no spacecraft could be used more than once.

Two booster rockets help to launch the shuttle (1).

At 28 miles, the boosters fall away and parachute back into the sea. They can then be rescued for use in future flights. The shuttle's main engines help it to reach a high enough speed to escape the earth's pull. The fuel tank then falls away (2).

In orbit, the shuttle is controlled by thruster rockets, as its wings do not work in space.

The crew set about their duties. On some flights, a satellite may be launched from the cargo bay (3).

When the mission is over the doors are shut and the shuttle prepares to return to earth. It hits the atmosphere at Mach 25, protected from the incredible heat by thousands of ceramic tiles all over its surface. Finally, it flies onto the runway like a glider (4).

Index